# After the Rain

## Ione W. Lyall

**Photography by Russ Busby**

Fleming H. Revell Company
Old Tappan, New Jersey

*Library of Congress Cataloging in Publication Data*
Lyall, Ione W
    After the rain.

    I. Title.
PS3562.Y3A7     811'.5'4     75-22068
ISBN 0-8007-0754-0

All photographs in the book are by Russ Busby except ''Ambassador Extraordinary'' which is a NASA photo.

To the memory of my dear husband
Andrew O. Lyall
whose fond dream before he left for
Glory-Land was that these poems should
go forth to whomsoever they might bless,
and
To our beloved sons Charles Andrew and Wallace McMillan
in whom I am well pleased

# Contents

# Acknowledgments

I thank God for leading me along this path He chose for me, and for the many wonderful people who through the years have walked beside me, giving me courage and inspiration to keep me climbing. I am indebted to R. Glenn Kershner D.M., acknowledged scientist, writer, and artist, who urged me to continue writing with confidence—especially poetry. Martha Snell Nicholson, it is now too late to thank you personally, but I shall seek you out in your Palace-of-Light.

To you, dear Dr. V. Raymond Edman, I appreciated more than I can tell the honor you extended me in 1966 when you requested some of my poems to use in your next inspirational book. But God called you Home before this could be realized.

Through more recent months and years I have had the privilege of knowing Lee Fisher, writer of books and songs as well as an evangelist connected with the Billy Graham Association, who has opened more than one gate for me. To him I shall ever be thankful.

I am deeply indebted to my dear friends Mildred and Fred Dienert for their active interest in getting my poems before the reading public.

During these exciting times Mary Frazer, realizing that I had need of a typist, and desiring to be a part of the project, time and again drove one hundred miles to spend days copying poems. Occasionally she found one which had no title as yet, and she was pleased to furnish it. I thank her.

Beloved Ruth Graham will never fully realize what her special interest through the years has meant, and what it always will mean—it is like inspiring music to my soul.

Quite recently a new possibility was given for my consideration by Russell Busby, well-known photographer. I was delighted to concur. Each of my poems is illustrated with a photo taken by Russ.

The gates have opened more readily than I could have supposed possible, strengthening my assurance that with God things do not just happen.

RUTH BELL GRAHAM

# Foreword

Years ago, as my husband was driving through Southern California, he suddenly came to the top of a ridge and looked down on what he considered the most beautiful little valley he had ever seen. In fact, he was so impressed with it that he later sent a friend back to ask more about it. Quite unexpectedly, the friend bumped into Andy and Ione Lyall, who lived in the valley and operated an orange grove there. Andy and Ione were not only fellow believers, but through radio and telecasts they were dear friends. Undiscovered on our part—but there.

It was shortly after this that Ione Lyall, who was deeply interested in a little school in Israel, stopped by to visit with me on one of her return trips. Though I had heard Bill speak of her, this was my first introduction to this warm, affectionate person whose loving faithfulness had led her husband to Christ, enabled her to raise two stalwart Christian sons, to establish a small Christian school halfway around the world, and still to have enough love to spill over to her neighbors and friends in her own local community.

Over the years her letters have been treasures. She writes as she talks: of the sun setting on Mount Palomar . . . the roadrunner raising a little family near a small adobe house in Pauma Valley . . . of the flowers, the trees and the birds that sing by day, and the coyotes that call by night. All were a part of her delightful letters, so I should not have been surprised when I found that Ione wrote poetry as well.

It is characteristic of Ione that she wrote for the sheer joy of writing: but for our sakes, I am delighted that at last she is sharing with us these beautiful bits and pieces of her own life.

RUTH B. GRAHAM

# Preface

The newly written poetry of our day has changed in style. No longer are patterns or rhymes necessary. Even capital letters and punctuation are ignored by some poets. I make a concession. Given a worthy experience of sight, sound, or inner "thoughts which breathe," I accept the author's choice of style.

As a small child I was taught the love of the Heavenly Father, and that every good and perfect gift comes from Him. He gave me the gift of observation plus the use of imagination which I began to use with a flow of attention at an early age. This began to demand expression as I noted the beauty of God's world about me—the sky, early spring violets, dragonfly wings. Soon I began to discover people—even myself—and this was interesting. When I learned to write, this expression sometimes drove me to the use of rhyme and rhythm. I sought out works of real poets. It was then that I began to appreciate the value of structure and choice of words. Through this stage I did not share this attitude, for I believed no one would be interested. Some attention was given my efforts in high school, with the result that I was chosen as class poet for graduation. In college I continued this line of study and again I was named class poet. People began to encourage me, not only in writing but also in sharing.

Recently, wonderful friends, not only persuaded, but led me to find the way of exposing my poems to the marketing of a book.

This collection is chosen from poems written through the years. It is not a biography, but often an experience lends itself to creation. A poet believes in the reality of imagination, and sometimes treats even the inanimate as though it had personality.

Different people find that different poems have different appeals. My prayer goes with this book that they who read its pages may find some blessing.

IONE WOOLPERT LYALL

ROSE—ROME, ITAL

# After the Rain

Today the seaborne wind brought rain
 Out of the scudding spindrift cloud.
It dimmed the winding dark-treed lane
 And hid the mountain in its shroud.

Heavy with drench the flaming rose
 Hung drooping on her thorny vine;
Beneath a thirsty dove came down
 To drink, and worship at its shrine.
Bright drops scattered as moody winds
 Shook the branches of the pine.

But now the sky is sapphire clear.
 The roving wind is freshly clean
And all the little clustering hills
 Are proudly wearing April green.

A solitary turtledove
 Has found a rainpool in the lane,
Green like the oak tree over head,
 Where he can dip, and dip again.

The air is faintly damp with scent
 Of purple lilac and wet sage
Scattered across the springtime slopes—
 The gift of last spring's heritage.

# Forever in My Heart

BLUEBIRD

Your gentle tears know naught of bitterness.
Wher'er you walk the crocus buds unfold.
Your smile, like warming sunlight, glows
    to bless
The home-return of early bluebirds, bold
Robins, and crested waxwings—brave to chart
Their flight in spite of winter's
    ling'ring cold.
I've loved you, April, from the very start,
And you shall live forever in my heart.

ROBIN

CROCUS

# April

April! When quickening branches volunteer
Their tender traceries against a sky
Grown brooding over somber, sleeping hills,
Clouds of young lamb's wool 'round their shoulders lest
They wake too early. April! When the cry
Of the crow sounds once again, tuneless and harsh
Above the naked fields and sodden marsh.

CHERRY BLOSSOMS—TOKYO, JAPAN

# Night Was a Lady

When I was very, very young
I liked to watch the night creep down
Out of the hills, and into town.
The trailing shadows were her skirts
Such as all lovely ladies wear;
And when the evening stars came out,
She wore bright diamonds in her hair.

FRAN

# August Mood

There is a new sound in the summer air.
I did not hear it as I trod the busy streets,
But, when I climbed the August hills
And stood to stare about me, it was there!
I cannot tell you what I heard;
It was as tho' an inner ear had ascertained
A hidden motif in the song
Of passing summer. Ripened grasses stirred,
And somewhere in the canyon sang a bird.

# Summer

Butterfly wings, and asters tall,
Rose petals drifting as they fall
From the rambler over the gray stone wall—
These go to make a summer.

# Late Winter Rains

All through the shortened days and lengthened nights
Of fall, and then December, west winds blew
But gently landward, never any clue
Of sea-born spawn of storm, nor even heights
Of pregnant clouds gave promise to our sight
Impatient for the drench long over due,
With January, apprehension grew.
Sad are the undamped hills 'till rain invites
The tender green, and latent buds awake.
The wild oat grass snaps sharply to proclaim
The softest tread of fawn across the brake.
The parched roots drain color from the flame
Of hollyberries ere their time. "Forsake
Not, God of Hills and Valleys, the just claim
Of Your own plantings. Consider them and slake
Before it be too late!" Then the rains came!

PAUMA VALLEY CHURCH

## Anchors

Today the west wind breathed upon the hills
  The salty scent of sunlit crested sea
Where toss the little ships of fishermen
  Near beds of kelp until the eventide.
And I who walked the winding
      hoof-marked trail,
Who know not weight of anchor steel—
      I heard
The lash of waves against the quiet beach,
  I saw the opalescent glow of sky and sea—

The ships that cross the far horizon, bound
   For ports around the world. I felt
      the tug
Of gravity that turns the tides, and knew
   The love of mariner for charting lanes
Across a boundless depth beneath the stars.
   I heard the cry of gulls, and my heart sang.
Yet followed I the winding hoof-marked trail,
   And knew the drag of anchor stronger far
Than weight of steel—the anchor of my heart.

TETON MOUNTAINS, WYOMING

# The Mountain Speaks

O you who strive in travail at my feet,
You who destroy yourselves, who without measure
Desire the riotous—making toil of pleasure.
Neighbor against neighbor you compete
For raiment which grows old, and for your meat
And drink. Thus is your mortal served. No leisure
For your weary minds and souls! Know you no treasure
In quietude and sacred inner joy? You greet
With anxious doubt and tension each new day.
Come, learn of me! The seasons ebb and flow,
Stars for the darkness, by day the sun to shine.
I stand unmoved by changes wrought. I know
The serene heritage of time is mine.
Let new storms lash! They, too, will pass away.

REDWOODS, CALIFORNIA

# Trees Are My Brothers

Trees are my brothers
Created by the same Master Hand.
When I am weak,
I stand among them.
Beholding their strength
Bred through resistance
In a thousand storms,
I, too, feel strong.
Yet, lean they with the wind,
As I must learn to lean
Without a broken wound,
When winds of fate breathe strong.
Hearing the proud songs they sing
Through twisted branches,
My heart sings;
Sings for the sense of beauty,
Beauty of rock, and green, and sky,
Beauty of resilience.
I feel my soul stretching upward
Even as the trees—
My brothers—reach toward God.

# Vast Lay the Tides

So vast lay the tides where the sea winds blew,
And white gulls flew
In wide sweeps
With pinioned grace—
Flew crying above the wet sands into
The bright wake where the low
Westing sun spread
Gleaming shards of polished copper hue.

    The vastness was a voice;
    The rhythm was a voice;
    The revel of color was a voice;
    And the voices sang to me
    A haunting, ringing melody.
    I thought, "You sing to me
    Of my heart's desire."

Let my love be vast as the swinging tide,
As deep, and wide.
May my love endure unstained as the snowy wing
Then God grant that it may bide
True, and free as the flight
Of the wild bird, asking nothing
Save its own bright fulfillment
    nought beside!

ATLANTIC OCEAN—LIBERIA, WEST AFRICA

# Reminder

Little harebell out of season growing,
 Blue spark of beauty in the golden grass,
Shall I pluck you and cut short your glowing,
Minute image of the soft October sky?
Or shall I gently touch your petals showing
 Above the green leaves of your pygmied stem,
Then, with prayerful reverence in my heart, knowing
 The grace and beauty of God's love, pass you by?

HAREBELL FROM SWITZERLAND

# Never a Dawn

My heart hurts for the world of men
Who know no tenderness of joy
Born with the newness of a spring,
Only stretch of fruitless days that bring
Bleakness to mind and soul—
Pain like the jagged lightning
Striking from the frightening
Drive of empty wind against
    the angry sky;
Men with in whom hope died cold—
Stillborn an illegitimate child of tyranny and greed;
Liege men of enslaved lands
Shackled by fears—men
Stripped of their dreams!
Never for them the dawn
    with gladdening light,
Nor spring,
Only stark winter, and the night.

KOREA

# I Never Shall Forget

Wherever I go I shall remember
    The sweeping glory of Palomar
    With her forested slopes of pine and fir;
    The sun-basked valley of Pauma Creek,
    And the tailored rows of orchards sleek
    In their glossy, dark-hued greens;
    The slanting meadows where neat holsteins
    Seek the shade of the live oak trees;
    The freshening coolness of the breeze
    Seaborne. I never shall forget
    The adobe house on the wooded hill,
    Nor the candle that waits on the windowsill.
    I shall fancy its light like a low star gleam
    Calling me back to my fond heart's dream.
    Over the sea and through the air,
    As straight as an arrow, as sure as prayer,
    Wherever I roam—I shall come back home.

THE LYALL HOME

PAUMA VALLEY,
CALIFORNIA

# I Know a Valley

Late lingers morning's gray upon the town,
The cooling dampness of the fog bears down
Across the restless harbor to the shore.
It spreads a well-worn blanket pierced by spires,
Muffling the mingled sounds of traffic roar,
Wrapping with wraithlike arms my heart's desires.

*I know a valley where the early sun*
*In spring spreads cloth of gold, and shadows run*
*Like long blue ribbons down the wooded slopes;*
*Where meadowlarks trill out their liquid lays,*
*And south winds whisper to the dreaming buds;*
*Where hours are woven into magic days.*

Come noon, I join the throngs down in the street
Where men walk close, nor ever deign to meet
With friendly look the folks who pass them by;
For each man in his own world walks alone.
We scarce look up to note the mist-cleared sky
Above the man-made canyon walls of stone.

*I know a valley, where the long road winds*
*Down from the peaceful hills, a road that finds*
*Its way through sun and shade, where dusty lanes*
*Lead off in friendly fashion—yawning—here*
*Mail boxes wait. No stranger passes by;*
*For every man's a neighbor far or near.*

Night follows closely on the heels of day.
The jostling crowds hurry to make their way,
Desiring each some respite for a while
From all the talk of wars; the urgent press;
Measuring effort by numbers on a dial;
The seething surge of man's deep restlessness.

*I know a valley where the quiet night*
*Falls like a benediction; where the light*
*Of rising moon over the tree-clad hills*
*Sends radiant mist across the countryside;*
*And every singing star bespeaks of God's*
*Eternal faithfulness wherein we bide.*

THE MOON

23

# Suburban Morning

City windows wake to see
Gray Dawn sneaking over the rooftops,
dragging his shadows with him,
barely escaping the surging flood of day;
a new day drawn to the pattern of yesterday
and faithful replica of all the tomorrows.

Down the street comes the milkman,
white-clad and driving a shining white truck.
Soft growl of motor and faint clinking
of glass against glass scarcely disturb
the drowsing air. The city windows blink
thru vague sticky sunlight to behold
bottles gleaming opaque on small porches.
Briefly the doors of the houses yawn
    and the bottles disappear.

Moments later people begin to spill
from the houses; men and women
clad for the factories and carrying lunches.
Follows a whang of garage doors, the muffled
start of reluctant motors; all in a trice
the street is alive with cars fretting to reach
the freeway before the green eye winks red.
And then a lull.

The city windows simply stare.
As far as they can see, roofs—some
hovering like gray partridges over
their coverts, some like sand cranes
obliquely motionless.

ATLANTA, GEORGIA

Soon the lull is over. Outbound are they,
in freshly creased apparel, who man
the freshly dusted desks and counters.
They also run, briefcases or handbags under arm.
Cautiously cars back out of driveways
Only to whirl, a multicolored eddy,
into the traffic stream. By eight o'clock
the tide again has ebbed.

# Montreux

Beyond the tulip trees
Shedding their petals on the grass,
The length and breadth of lake—
The gray-blue waters of Leman
Shifting its silver shards
Brighter than a million stars
Out of a moonless night.

Beyond the lake
The mountains rise,
Their jagged snowy peaks
Stretching sharply up and up
Thru shadows, faintly gray,
Of clouds. They pierce the sky
Over the clouds to snatch
The glory of the Alpine sun.

But now the clouds drop off
The shoulders of the regal Midi
Just as a scarf slips down.
Borrowing bright glory from
The sun, the snow slopes send
Long reflections faintly glowing
From her shore across to mine.

Blue of the sky,
Shadows of blue,
Blue of the lake,
White of the snows,
Gold of the sun!
All in an hour wonders unfold
Till no more of splendor, Creator, Lord,
Can my heart hold!

MONTREUX, SWITZERLAND

# The House on the Hill

Yes, a lady keeps that house on the hill.
She grows window boxes on every sill.
She sweeps the stepping-stones past the great
Weeping willow to her small white gate.
She trims the roses, and ties the stalks
Of the leaning larkspur and hollyhocks.
I've seen her grin at the pansy faces,
And gently touch the Queen Anne's laces,
Now and then she peers at the purple hills,
Wistful—like she was wishing for daffodils,
Even tho' she knows it's approaching fall;
For she said one time, "First of all
Next year I shall plant me rows of gold
Daffodils—all my yard can hold!
For I love spring! I am tuned to spring!
And a daffodil just makes my heart sing!"

When the Delicious got ripe I took three or four
And I knocked right gentle on her front door.
She came, and she opened the door real wide,
With a friendly nod, and I saw inside.
Every thing was in order; everything shone.
Being curious, I asked, "Do you live here alone?"
"Yes sir," she said. "Far as mortal can see,
But I have my family of Dreams," said she.
Everything was trim in its proper space,
But it had the good look of a lived-in place.
It was my desire to stop a while,
But I was dismissed with "Thanks," and a smile,
So I took me back thru the picket gate
And down the road with reluctant gait.

Just a couple weeks back I heard at the inn
That a stranger arrived. Where he had been
And where he was going nobody knows,
Nor even his name; but the story goes
That he rode right thru the small white gate,
And he tethered his roan for an hour's wait
Beneath the weeping willow tree,
(As pretty a roan as you'd wish to see!)
Now what was talked of no one would know,
But Malcolm the Weaver just happened to go
That way as the stranger was fixing to leave,
And he asked the lady had she aught to weave.

She listened to his quiet speech,
Something of "rights," Malcolm said, and each

Seemed moved in a peculiar way;
Mysterious it was, but I would say
No doubt it made sense to the two of them.
Well—it's in my mind that she shall not clem,
With my root house full, and with meat to spare—
Tho' she may be proud, and loathe to share.

But, since that day, she hasn't been seen
In the garden; yet it is still swept clean
And the roses and hollyhocks nod and sway
In the frisking breeze in the same old way.
Nor has anyone seen her in the town.
Her house looks asleep with its shades pulled down.
Can it possibly be that she followed a whim,
And rode away with the likes of *him?*

# Old Bell

Old bell, old bell—a century of years
you've sung your song from your shelter on the slope.
Padres have come and gone. They bade you sing,
and then they went their way along the trails.

But still you hear the twittering of birds
in branches of the eucalyptus. Still
you watch the dark-skinned children play
through the sunlit hours.

You guard your secrets well—the tryst beneath
the stars of lovers; tales of age-old men
whose halting steps have trod the worn path at your feet.
Roses have bloomed, and fallen forgotten
since you sang of little human buds who drooped
and died a hundred years ago.

Still you call the humble ones to worship,
and on occasion, greet the happy bride;
or, in sad tones, announce departure of some soul
    heaven bound.
Through long days you slumber unmolested,
in the season of blue grapes; of mellow amber light;
or when crimson peppers dry, ruddying the landscape.
Sometime I wonder—what are the dreams you dream!

MISSION ESPADA—SAN ANTONIO, TEXAS

# Drumlin-by-the-Sea

I know just how the night comes down
   O'er Drumlin-by-the-Sea.
The sea gulls furl their wings of gray
On rocky reefs at close of day,
Where tossing bell buoys dodge and play
   Near Drumlin-by-the-Sea.

I've seen the eucalyptus trees,
   In Drumlin-by-the-Sea,
Turn ebon 'gainst the fading sky.
I've heard the low and windful cry
Of myriad pipers passing by
   Near Drumlin-by-the-Sea.

PACIFIC OCEAN, CALIFORNIA COAST

I've seen the sharp star-points prick thru
   O'er Drumlin-by-the-Sea.
I've watched the gold-washed moon ride in
On the ghostful boat which may have been
But the shimmery path *you* oft have seen
   From Drumlin-by-the-Sea.

So does the clinging night come down
   To Drumlin-by-the-Sea.
The quaint old climbing streets, which run
'Twixt vine-wreathed doors that face the sun,
Have welcomed sleep when day is done
   In Drumlin-by-the-Sea.

# Faith

Today up in a windy sky
I saw a white bird flying.
Bright were his wings against the gray
Of heavy clouds, his winged way
Straight as a shaft went plying.

God, make my faith like that white bird,
Bravely to soar unerring,
Gleaming pure white like a single ray
Against the threat of a stormy day
Without a cry, forth faring!

SEA GULL—COPENHAGEN, DENMARK

HAIFA, ISRAEL

# Destiny

The sun sank low in the cloud bank
    At the western rim of the sea.
I left your shores, O Israel,
    With a pain in the heart of me;
Pain for your brave ones of every age,
    Mothers whose sons went forth
To one battlefront or another—
    East, west, south or north;
Fronts of danger by day or night
    Where spewed the bullets of hate—
Tanks, guns, and always men
    Hiding in hills, lying in wait

For death. To give or receive—
    According to their destiny,
Fathers gave of their lifeblood
    Which coursed thru the veins of their sons;
Children scarce born; and the small ones
    Playing at war with toy guns;
Wives, struggling with misgiving,
    Sent full sacrifice of the living,
Yet, with what pride in the giving!
    Youth—teeming with youth—
The boys and the girls of yesterday—
    Today grown into uniform, saying,
"Even for such a time as this was I born!"
From the land that night came your songs.
    I left your shores in the sunset glow—
Haifa with lights on the mountain slopes
    And I said, thru my pain, "Tho' I go,
Surely here a part of my heart belongs!"
God of Ages, born and unborn,
God of the covenants with
                  Your chosen ones,
For their sake—
            Remember Israel, We pray
And bring them into the Bright New Day!

SUNSET IN JERUSALEM

# The Eve of Betrayal

Judas Iscariot, is it the thin whispering
Of the chill wind through the olive leaves
Which unnerves you?
Or is it the starkness of the silver-plated moon
Over low-slung hills?
Or is it the stillness of shadows slowly creeping
Among swaying trees that disturbs your spirit?

   Ah, the warm feel of His flesh as I kissed Him!
   The yielding warmth of His flesh as I kissed Him!
   Be still, my heart! Was He not an imposter?

Quicken, Judas, quicken your steps.
Let them take you far from this trampled garden;
Away from the flickering lanterns and torches;
Away from the voices of the rabble.
Better to follow the moon-washed road alone—
The winding pebbly moon-washed road—
Back to the streets of the town.

30 PIECES OF SILVER FRANCIAN MUSEUM, JERUSALEM

Yea, they were the rabble!
Jehovah! How I shall always hate
The light of a torch in a garden!
I said, "Hail, Master!" And then I kissed Him.
Would that my ears had not heard
The reproach of the voice, as though He were God,
Divinely gentle, yet infinitely powerful.
But I am a man of shrewdness. Should I believe
**That one who sated His mortal hunger**
From the same bowl with me is likely
To be the very Son of God?

And so you would flee from your torment, Judas,
You with your little fears of whispering leaves,
Of moonlight pale as death,
Of shadows that smother your shrinking soul!
Think you that you can forget this night?
Though you live to be old as the stars themselves,
Though you breathe as endlessly
As the wind from over the Great Sea,
Though your blood course as staunchly
As the Jordan River,
Yet shall you ever remember the feel of warm flesh,
And that voice which will grow to fill
All of earth, and heaven beside!
You will remember how—first by inclination,
And then by word and deed—you betrayed the Innocent One
For love of silver!
You did not know you loved silver, Judas?
So does the unwanted seed germinate unseen,
And, all untended, spread its strangling roots.
Lo, neither may you be forgotten,
For henceforth you shall lend your name
To all committing base betrayal.
Go, Judas, tread the pebbled moon-washed road.
Neither the whispering wind, nor the ashen moonlight,
Nor the somber shadow can hurt you.
Go—laugh in the town, and spend
Your thirty pieces of silver!

Thirty pieces of silver! It was not enough!
No doubt the chief priests would have paid
Much higher, but I was willing then
To covenant for thirty pieces of silver.
For thirty pieces of silver I sold myself!
Still I can see those eyes!
They bored deep into the secret place of my soul.
I stood naked before Him, unclothed even by my flesh!
He said, "Friend, wherefore art thou come?"
He called me friend!
I sold Him to His certain death; yet,
Yet I am persuaded that death cannot hold the Man.
Did He not declare He would live again?
Yea, it is I who died!
When morning comes I will find those priests;
I will return their silver.
But never in all God's eternity
Can I take back the kiss!

# I Thank Thee

In all the springs I hold within my memory
I've never seen the sudden burst of almond bloom
So purely white against the backdrop of the blue
Of shadowed mountain slope—like spray of driven spume.

I think that never have the winds so gentle been
To drift the clouds with featheredges softly curled;
Nor ever have the golden trumpets of the dawn
Sounded so proud a prelude to the waiting world.

I had forgotten, if I ever knew, how charmed
Can be the cadence of the silver drip of rain;
How sweet the scent of heather heavy with the dew;
How misty green the sycamores along the lane.

Whether in truth this year has brought a lovelier spring,
Or if it is but in my heart, I do not know.
I only know if LOVE can make of earth a heaven
Then, God, I thank Thee for this LOVE that makes it so.

LEXINGTON, KENTUCKY

# Only Forgotten Love

The mist lies over the heather, lass;
Like a kirtle the mist wraps my heart around.
Before today has spent its way
We'll have said farewell. I'll mind the sound

Of the pounding, and crash of the sullen sea—
And the bursting beat of the heart of me—
And the mist, and rain, and the bruising pain
Of our parting—no matter where I be!

Yet I must go, and you must stay.
It seems ever so in this world, my Love!
The rainbow fades; and in the glades
The darkness smothers the song of the dove.

So give me your kiss as a token, lass,
And bear me a thought as the days go by,
For I will be true in remembering you.
'Tis only forgotten love can die!

DAVID AND CAROL

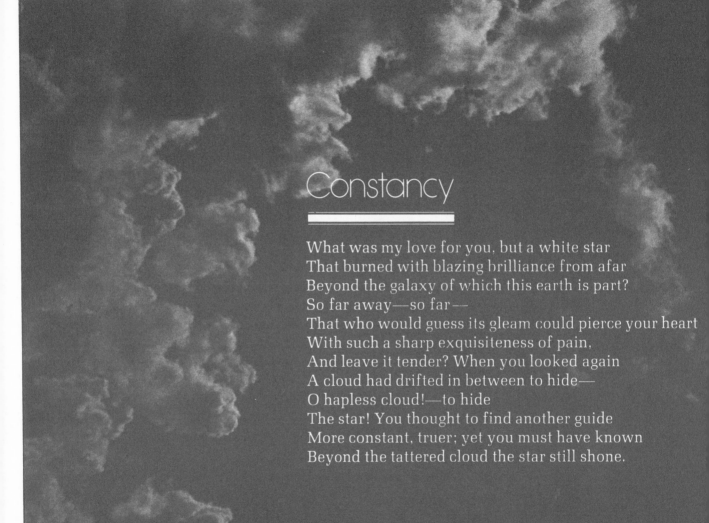

# Constancy

What was my love for you, but a white star
That burned with blazing brilliance from afar
Beyond the galaxy of which this earth is part?
So far away—so far—
That who would guess its gleam could pierce your heart
With such a sharp exquisiteness of pain,
And leave it tender? When you looked again
A cloud had drifted in between to hide—
O hapless cloud!—to hide
The star! You thought to find another guide
More constant, truer; yet you must have known
Beyond the tattered cloud the star still shone.

# Mary Louise

"Mary Louise, come stir up your batter.
    The hired man's here with new milk sloppin' over;
    The bees have begun sippin' down in the clover.
    Come, Mary Louise! Be a helpin' of Mother!"
"Yes, Mother, I'm coming," laughs Mary Louise.

"Mary Louise, come here for the minute!
    'Tis bothered I am to be finding my knitting.
    I was sure that I laid it close where I was sitting.
    There—how can I thank you with words most befitting?"
"Now, Gran, I love you," smiles Mary Louise.

"Mary Louise, I've hurted my finger.
    I borrowed the knife only just for a minute;
    I didn't suppose there was any harm in it.
    But you'll wrap it all up in white cloth, and pin it?"
"Sure, Brother, I'll fix it," says Mary Louise.

"Mary Louise, I'm down by the locust!
    The new moon is touching the hill with her finger;
    The crickets are tuning; the linnets still linger
    To sing a last note. My heart's all a-hunger!"
"Yes, Loved One, I'll be there," breathes Mary Louise.

Mary Louise, can you know how I miss you!
    The gold of the sunshine has lost all its brightness;
    The lilt of the breeze has no longer its lightness;
    And nothing I do can have any rightness.
Can God need you more than I, Mary Louise?

# Nostalgia

I would that I might reach my hand,
And with a choice at my command,
Select from out the magic bag
Of memory's well-worn rag and tag,
Something to hold within my grasp—
Something to treasure in my clasp.

For, now that I have older grown,
I look back o'er the years I've known,
And wonder why that far-off day
Seems fraught with charm, and blissful, gay
Enchantment. Even the rain cloud's spill
Left a rainbow poised on every hill.
In the wooded glade at the early morn.
One glimpsed the golden unicorn.

There was never a heavy-gaited hour
From dawn to curfew. Each season's dower
Furnished enough, and to spare, of joy
To regale the spirit of any boy.
Yet all earth's substance could not pay
For the glad content of childhood's day.

# God and She

She knew God even before she was six.
That was the year she lost her shoe,
And she talked to God, and God found
    it where
The puppy had dragged it under the blue
Lilac bush.
       And then she remembered the time
The kitten got stepped on HARD by the mule,
How its legs got limp so it couldn't run,
And it looked at you hurt just something cruel!
       But she prayed, and the kitten got all well.

There was the day that she had found
The teensiest yellow violet
Hid in its leaves on the wet spring ground,
Out of the cold brown earth it had come.
When she asked her mother how violets grew
She was told God makes them, spring beauties,
Wood trilliums, and jack-in-the-pulpits, too.

CAROLYN ANNE

And God makes babies, so Aunt Beth said.
He cares for the birds, and He paints the sky.
In fact He made the whole big world;
He hung every one of the stars up high.
But the best of all was the cozy feel
Like the warmth that the glowing coal fire sends
All through the room on a winter's night,
The feeling that God and she were *Friends!*

# Mother

What do I owe my mother?
Countless things I could not name,
A thousand ingrained hopes and aims,
The love of all things beautiful,
The stars at night and snowflakes
Softly falling from a winter's sky—
The love of books with all the joy that comes
From reading by a happy fire.
Through her eyes I learned
To see the streak of humor
That lies, an almost hidden thread,
In Life's bright, tangled skein.
To have a care for others,
To find pleasure in the kindly tho't or word
That leaves a warmer heart behind.
To keep above all else
A keen delight in life itself,
An eagerness for all that life can give.
Toward building happiness.
These things and many more are mine,
Because you, Mother, put them in my heart.
What words have I
        to truly frame
The tribute that
        my love would
            bring?

# Leah in Chapel

How often I have watched you there
    Upon your little chapel chair!
First you loosed—and tied each shoe.
    Just for something else to do,
You smoothed your apron, ruffles and all.
    You drew from out its pocket small
A piece of string—a short piece. This
    You rolled about, stopping to kiss
The small finger you hurt yesterday.

Quite suddenly you were aware
Of all the children's voices sweet
Singing a hymn, filling the air,
But then the voice of the teacher came,
So back you slipped to your dreams again.
You dropped small hands upon your lap,
Palms up, to make a little bowl.

TRACY

I saw the wonder and surprise
That looked from out your big brown eyes,
To think you held a dish of gold!
Hands held with care lest it should spill,
    You lifted up your gaze until
You saw the sunlight streaming through
    The window by the green fir tree,
A warm and lovely thing to see!

(What if you could hold it tight
    Forever and forever bright!
Did we suppose, were WE so bold
    as to think you always could hold the gold?)
I watched you slowly close your hands,
    To see if all of the gold was there,
When you opened them again.

                                    It was!!!

# My Little Son

Heart of me, soul of me,
    My little son—
Tired of your toys
    When day is done,

Come to your mother.
    Her arms are your nest.
Dear little birdling,
    Sleep on my breast.

Dark is a-coming,
    Stars peeping out;
Night breeze a-humming
    Softly about.
I hear the dream-man
    With sandy tread
Coming to see if
    You're in your bed.

Feet that are weary
    From trudging all day,
Hands that are grimy
    And dirty from play,

Lips that have prattled,
    Eyes that have smiled,
Dearer than life to me
    Is my sweet child.

Rainbows of promise
    Have glistened thru tears.
Bright may they gleam
    Thru passing years.
Manhood is coming.
    Some dawning day
Will find you forgetting
    Your toys laid away.

The nest will be empty,
    And lonely, and still.
No more will the sandman
    Come over the hill.
But still I shall feel you
    When day is done,
Safe in my arms,
    My little son.

KEVIN

KEV

# Observations

I think kitten's paws are the softest, cutest things,
And big dragonflies have the shimmeringest wings.

Golden-brown toadstools are the smoothest things I know;
Teensy blue wood violets are the sweetest things that grow.

Now the thing most quiet is the shadow on the grass
When it moves on over just to let the sunshine pass.

Ask me what's the highest in the world, I'll tell you true—
It's the steeple towering from the church. It hits the blue

Sky that hides the place where the angels live with God.
Next to highest must be my Grandpapa's lightning rod.

But if you should wonder how about the nicest things
I'd name two bests—listening to the songs that Papa sings

When the day is dark'ning; and the other one is this—
Mother bending over for my sleepy good-night kiss.

# The Inward Sight

Fresh were the winds when he put to sea,
    And white were the sails spread wide.
Bright was the sun on the yellow sand
    Washed clean by the singing tide.

Loud were the cries of the wheeling gulls,
    And loud was my beating heart.
Salt were my tears as the salty sea—
    Such pain did it cost to part.

Wide is the sea, and wide the sky.
    Full many a day I'll bide
Outwardly gay, but with secret fear
    That gnaws with keen tooth inside.

Yet when I pray it is given to me
    That love has an inward sight—
Faith, some may name it. I only know
    It looks through the darkest night.

Some joyous morning when fresh winds blow
    I'll stand by the tossing sea.
Sure as a bird with her wings outspread,
    Far out will the good ship be.

How shall I know? By the set of sail,
    And by the proud way she rides
Bearing him home! For my eyes shall *see*,
    But there's Love's inward sight besides.

MRS. GRAHAM

EARTH FROM SPACE (NASA PHOTO

# Ambassador Extraordinary

Love shaped a world and swung it in celestial space,
Wrapped it by day in diaphanous blue in which to trace
Patterns of clouds; by night in garment richly spun
Of velvet black, embroidered thick with stars—
The moon a lamp; by day the light of sun.

Love fashioned then a crystal drop of rain, and so
The clouds might water all the earth; carved flakes of snow;
Painted the mountains, and the plains, the desert sand—
Here piney green, there granite blue, or stretch of gold—
And circumscribed with ceaseless ocean tides the land.

Howbeit neither on the plain nor mountainside,
Not yet within a desert place does Love abide.
Ambassador, who once the streets of Heaven trod,
He searches out the willing human heart for home,
That man, despite his feet of clay, may walk with God.

# If I Could Only Sing One Song

If I could only sing one song,
    And all the world might understand,
I'd sing of FAITH, a light that glows,
And in the darkness brighter grows;
    A faith with no more questioning
    Than the gold cup raises to the sun;
    Or the mighty eagle on the wing
    To the air which bears his weight. Not one
    Long miracle was ever wrought
    In heaven or earth except 'twere brought
    About thru Faith of God or man,
        Since time began.
I'd sing of Faith to make hearts strong
If I could only sing one song.

# Hold My Hand

Lord, You understand!
    You heard the crash like sudden doom
    You saw the fear-dilated eyes
    of my soul survey the ground where lay
    the gloom-wrapped pieces of my hopes,
    shattered in less time than it could take
    a second hand to round the dial.

    Lord, You know the agony
    of a broken heart, and so,
    Dear Lord, please—hold my hand.

REBECCA

# Communion

I thank Thee, Lord, for planting in my heart
These needs—yea these desires:
Arbutus, pale and lovely with the glow
Of flushing sunrise underneath the snow;
The freshening feel of wind upon my face,
The movement of bare branches, full of grace;
The sight of children playing in the sun,
The satisfaction of a task well done.

I trust that I shall never grow too old
To thrill with glad surprise when I behold
The simple things of beauty close to me,
A rainbow in the sky, a dogwood tree;
The incense of the pines, the sharp outline
Of frosty, silver-plated firs that shine
Gray 'gainst the winter sky o'erhead, below,
The pure and seamless garment of the snow.

SNOW—MINNESOTA

I pray Thee, Lord, that I may ever hold
These things immutable;
A FAITH that shall not lose its power of flight
For want of exercise, a faith with might
To wing its way up to the farthest sun,

Or wait with patience till the prize is won;
HOPE, an untarnished lantern in my hand
That I may boldly walk, nor fear to stand
Alone in times of stress. Perchance its ray
May light a fellow pilgrim on his way.
And LOVE, the crowning grace, which multiplies
Good unto the beloved, nor yet denies
Full measure to the giver. Let me then
Feel that my life is justified.    Amen.

# God's Radio

One day as God sat in His Palace of Light
    He fingered His radio dial.
"I've listened to Gabriel's trumpet solo,
    Now I'll tune in on earth for a while.
Oh, yes, here's a station that's good, I am sure.
    I've been answ'ring their prayers about rain."
"The weather is murkey and muggy down here!
    The weeds are all starting again!"
"Oh, dear, where's another? I'll try for the place
    Where the folks have been asking for sun.
What is this?" "Weather torrid—our crops will be burned
    Ere the season for harvest's begun!"
"I don't care for that. Let me see—how is this?"
    "Our trials are irking us sore.
We wish we might now from all worries be free!"
    ("They were praying for patience before—

There's no pleasure in listening now to that tune.")
    "We need gold that our debts we may pay.
Send us work. Then we'll praise You forever, Oh, God!
    And we'll give you the glory for aye."
Next another discord sadly smote on His ear;
    "We have plenty of gold, to be sure!

DAN AND BRUCE

But the preachers and relatives beg for our gold,
   While our work is too hard to endure.''
"And so on, and so on!" (So sadly God spoke.)
   "Not a word of thanksgiving I hear.
I answer their prayers, yet they only complain.
   They WILL NOT be happy, I fear.
Ah, listen to this! I find music at last
   In the sweet little voice of a child!"
"Dear God, I'm so thankful for ALL that You send—
   I KNOW You will bless me!" God smiled.

# Matins

Thou shalt love the Lord thy God with all thy heart,
and with all thy soul, and with all thy mind. Matthew 22:37

Praise Him who is worthy of praise, my heart!
    For the dawn of creation that lingers still
    In the blush of the rose on the brow of my hill;
    In the swirling mists that linger late;
    In the newborn lamb at my pasture gate.

Praise Him who is worthy of praise, my soul!
    For the heaven-born miracle of grace
    Which makes me an inheritor. The face
    Of the mountains, the vaulted sky, the sea,
    All hills, and the rivers belong to me.

Praise Him who is worthy of praise, my mind!
    For the infinite wisdom whose revenue
    Is better than silver, yet even the new
    Fledgling dove, in good time, will have wisdom to fly
    Without compass or load where her little ones lie.

TEN THOUSAND FEET ABOVE THE U.S.A.

# God Grant

God grant that I may not forgetful grow
Of qualities of virtue man can know
From closeness to the mountains and the sky,
From living trees, and from the winds that blow.
For in that world to which the long road leads,
Each day brings forth the challenge of those needs
Common to mankind since the world began.
Persistent trial and proving mark the plan
Of cycles each must run, with something more
Than courage and resolve to win the score.

Then, whether winds that blow be foul or fair,
Give me the strength and resilience of pine.
Let me know calm and dignity of soul
Above the gusty turmoil, and resign
Me to a greater good than I can see—
A part of the Creator's own design.

# Evening Prayer

I look to the mellow of sunset glow
    That sharpens the edge of the western slope;
    I watch the blue shadows silently grope
Thru the hills where the freshening sea winds blow.

Dimly the stars venture out overhead.
    Down thru my valley the soothing night
    Treads quietly after the garish light
Of the care-filled day. Like a silver thread

The veriest moon hangs low till it dips.
    Gone too is the hurt of day-born scars
    As I reach to the Lord of the earth and stars,
With a prayer of thankfulness on my lips.